Unlocking the Secrets of Science

Profiling 20th Century Achievers in Science, Medicine, and Technology

Oswald Avery and the Story of DNA

Vesta-Nadine Severs and Jim Whiting
with Review by Dr. Deni Galileo

Mitchell Lane
PUBLISHERS

PO Box 619
Bear, Delaware 19701

Unlocking the Secrets of Science

Profiling 20th Century Achievers in Science, Medicine, and Technology

Oswald Avery and the Story of DNA

. . . .

Second Printing

Library of Congress Cataloging-in-Publication Data
Severs, Vesta-Nadine and Jim Whiting.
    Oswald Avery and the story of DNA/Vesta-Nadine Severs and Jim Whiting.
        p. cm. —(Unlocking the secrets of science)
    Includes bibliographical references and index.
    Summary: A biography of the Canadian-born bacteriologist whose research on pneumonia and other bacteria led to a new understanding of DNA which, in turn, led to DNA fingerprinting in criminal investigation, paternity testing, and genetic engineering.
    ISBN 1-58415-110-2
    1. Avery, Oswald Theodore, 1877-1955—Juvenile literature. 2. Bacteriologists—Biography—Juvenile literature. 3. Physicians—Biography—Juvenile literature. 4. DNA—History—Juvenile literature. 5. Bacterial transformation—History—Juvenile literature. [1. Avery, Oswald Theodore, 1877-1955. 2. Bacteriologists. 3. Physicians. 4. DNA—History.] I. Title. II. Series.
QR31.A9 S48 2001
579.3'092—dc21
    [B]   2001038710

ABOUT THE AUTHORS: Vesta-Nadine Severs is a freelance writer whose articles have appeared in more than 60 newspapers and magazines from the United States to Taiwan to India. Her non-fiction has appeared in publications such as *Boys' Life* and *Sirs, Mandarin, Inc.* Her young adult novel, *Lucinda*, received an award in an Oklahoma Writers Federation contest. Ms. Severs has taught writing in five schools in Missouri and is a frequent speaker at public libraries and in schools. **Jim Whiting** has been a journalist, writer, editor, and photographer for more than 20 years. In addition to a lengthy stint as publisher of *Northwest Runner* magazine, Mr. Whiting has contributed articles to the *Seattle Times*, *Conde Nast Traveler*, *Newsday*, and *Saturday Evening Post*. He has edited more than 20 titles in the Mitchell Lane Real-Life Reader Biography series and Unlocking the Secrets of Science. He holds a B.A. degree in philosophy and an M.A. degree in English. He lives in Washington state with his wife and two teenage sons.

ABOUT THE REVIEWER: Dr. Deni Galileo reviewed this book for scientific accuracy and clarity. He received his Ph.D. degree from the University of Florida College of Medicine. He is currently an Assistant Professor of Biological Sciences at the University of Delaware. He received postdoctoral training at Washington University School of Medicine and was formerly on the faculty of the Medical College of Georgia. Dr. Galileo studies molecules and mechanisms that control migration of neuronal cells in the early developing vertebrate brain and uses multiple microscopical and molecular biological techniques, including recombinant DNA.

PHOTO CREDITS: pp. 6, 10, 21, 22, 26, 30 The Rockefeller University Archives; pp. 16, 34 Science Photo Library; p. 38 AP Photo.

PUBLISHER'S NOTE: In selecting those persons to be profiled in this series, we first attempted to identify the most notable accomplishments of the 20th century in science, medicine, and technology. When we were done, we noted a serious deficiency in the inclusion of women. For the greater part of the 20th century science, medicine, and technology were male-dominated fields. In many cases, the contributions of women went unrecognized. Women have tried for years to be included in these areas, and in many cases, women worked side by side with men who took credit for their ideas and discoveries. Even as we move forward into the 21st century, we find women still sadly underrepresented. It is not an oversight, therefore, that we profiled mostly male achievers. Information simply does not exist to include a fair selection of women.

Contents

Dr. Oswald Theodore Avery, dedicated scientist, was a soft spoken and very shy man. He rarely accepted any of the social invitations he received.

Chapter 1

A Case for DNA Fingerprinting

· ·

On September 17, 1994, Ron Williamson was moved to a special holding cell at the State Penitentiary in McAlester, Oklahoma for condemned prisoners having less than a week to live. Most of the inmates on his section were glad that he was gone, as Williamson had been screaming day and night until hoarse, "I'm innocent! I'm innocent! I did not kill Debra Carter!"

Debra Carter was a young woman who had been brutally murdered nearly twelve years earlier. She worked at a night club which Williamson and a friend, Dennis Fritz, often visited.

Williamson was soon picked up for questioning and took polygraph tests. He angrily denied having anything to do with Debra Carter's murder. His fingerprints didn't match the few that were found at the scene of the crime, and his mother told police that her son had been home in bed by 10:00 on the evening of the murder. Fritz, also questioned by the police, denied being an accomplice just as strongly. Neither Williamson, a former minor league baseball player, nor Fritz had ever been in serious trouble with the law.

Several years went by and no one had been charged with Debra Carter's murder. But the police were closing in.

In jails there are often "snitches," people already in jail who claim to have heard other inmates confess crimes. They pass on this information to police in the expectation that they will receive a lighter or shortened sentence. A woman who had been imprisoned in the county jail said she heard a confession by Williamson when he was first questioned. Similarly, a jail employee said he'd heard the same thing from Fritz.

In addition, some stray hairs that had been taken from the victim had finally been linked to Williamson and Fritz by an expert from the state crime laboratory who examined them under the microscope, using methods commonly accepted at that time.

A man named Glen Gore also testified that he saw Williamson with the victim the night she died. He was the only witness to connect them.

Both men were brought to trial and the jury found them guilty. Fritz received a life sentence while Williamson was sentenced to death. Seven years later he was transferred to the special holding cell on Death Row and told that he had less than a week to live.

But two days later, a federal court issued a stay of execution. Eventually Williamson received a new attorney, Mark Barrett.

Barrett did a much better job of representing Ron Williamson. He showed that his client had a history of mental problems that had not been brought out at the trial. He revealed that the jailhouse snitch was a repeat offender who had passed on similar stories about other inmates. And he pointed out that even though Gore—who was Debra Carter's boyfriend at one time—was a man with a long criminal history who had refused to testify in person at the trial, his written testimony had been admitted as evidence.

But all his good work still might not have released Ron Williamson if it had not been for one thing: DNA "fingerprinting."

What is DNA fingerprinting? To answer that question, we need to look at the structure of our bodies. Every human being is made up of trillions of tiny microscopic cells, many of which have specialized functions such as muscle cells, nerve cells, skin cells, and so on. But all cells have one thing in common: they all contain a center portion which is called the nucleus.

Part of the nucleus is made up of long, thin, rod-like strands which are called chromosomes. These carry the material that determines our heredity, and we get half our chromosomes from each parent. Chromosomes, in turn, consist of individual genes. And genes are composed of DNA, or deoxyribonucleic acid, which contains the actual "blueprint" that determines virtually everything about a person, from hair color to height.

DNA is an extremely long and complex molecule, and no two people have exactly the same DNA. It is therefore as unique as our fingerprints. It only takes a small sample of DNA from a person's blood or skin to make a DNA fingerprint.

So Williamson and Fritz underwent DNA testing. Because he believed so strongly in Ron Williamson's innocence, it came as no big surprise to Barrett that the DNA from the hairs which were found on Debra Carter's body didn't match the samples that had been taken from either his client or from Dennis Fritz. What may have surprised him was the identity of the person it did match: Glen Gore.

Gore was eventually charged with the crime while Williamson and Fritz were released. After 12 years in prison they were free men because of their DNA tests. Williamson and Fritz owed a great deal to the many scientists who had discovered DNA and eventually released its secrets, although it's highly unlikely that the two men knew the names of any of those dedicated people whose research had resulted in their release.

"Ossie," as his family called him, put "his hand through the gate" of education. He always made excellent grades.

Chapter 2

Putting a Hand Through the Gate

● ●

One of most important of the scientists whose work on DNA had long-reaching effects, was a small man born in Canada named Oswald Avery. He grew up playing the cornet and didn't even decide that he was going to go into science until he graduated from college. He spent most of his life doing laboratory work, and his most famous discovery wasn't fully recognized or appreciated while he was still alive.

While Avery didn't actually discover DNA fingerprinting, his research provided a vital steppingstone along the process. And his story illustrates one of the most important facts about scientific discoveries: they don't just come out of the blue, but depend on the work of many men and women who precede the actual discoverer.

In the city of Halifax in the Canadian province of Nova Scotia, British emigrants Joseph and Elizabeth Avery gave birth to their second son, Oswald Theodore Avery, on October 21, 1877.

Oswald's father was a popular and successful minister in the Baptist church, and for his first 10 years, young Oswald grew up in a stable environment. His life centered around attending school and the church his father helped to found, which was called The Tabernacle. A small, sturdy boy, Oswald began helping his father with church activities at an early age.

Oswald's life changed dramatically in 1887, when Joseph received an invitation to become pastor at a mission church called the Mariners' Temple in New York City's Lower East Side. From the clean fresh air of the ocean, the family—

which now consisted of three sons, as Roy had been born two years earlier—was plunged into an environment that could scarcely have been more different from what they'd been accustomed to. The streets were very crowded, while poverty, drunkenness and fighting were common. It was all very different from what young Oswald had known.

"People, people everywhere," Oswald's mother Elizabeth said in René Dubos' biography of Avery, *The Professor, The Institute, and DNA.* "Crowded into lofty tenement houses, burrowing in basements, packed in cheap lodging-houses, and swarming on the streets. Even to the ordinary Christian worker the situation is one that would seem to defy all effort to improve it. Vice in a hundred repulsive forms holds many in its iron grasp."

The family found the local Baptist community to be close-knit even in the midst of the poverty and squalor of the city. The Averys made every effort toward making their church into a busy place for religious and social activities.

They quickly encountered one problem: the church organ was so dilapidated that it couldn't be played. Because Mrs. Avery believed that music was an important element in church services, she found a young man who played the cornet—an instrument similar to a trumpet, only a little smaller—and talked him into performing.

It didn't take long for both Oswald—who was also known by his nickname of Ossie—and his older brother Ernest to become interested in the instrument. They found an old one and taught themselves to play. The young musician gave them free lessons and before he was 12 Oswald was playing regularly, both in Sunday School and at regular services. Not only that, both boys also played their cornets on the steps of the Mariners' Temple on Sunday afternoons to attract passersby to the worship services.

In addition to his direct responsibilities, Joseph Avery edited a church newspaper called "Buds and Blossoms" and apparently had some medical experience. He patented a preparation called "Avery's Auraline," which was for "relief and cure of deafness, earaches and noises in the head."

Life wasn't easy for the family, because Reverend Avery didn't make much money. But the Baptist community was always willing to help out, as they did when the Averys' home burned down in 1890. The rebuilding effort received an additional boost with a check for $100 from the richest man in the world, John D. Rockefeller, who was a strong believer in the Baptist faith. In addition to helping the Averys directly, he also contributed money on a regular basis to the Mariners' Temple.

Later that year, on December 30, the Averys received a letter from Rockefeller, which no doubt made the season very special for them. Rockefeller sent another check—this one for $50, still a lot of money in those days—and included an invitation for the family to go ice skating in the Rockefellers' back yard, which was flooded during the cold winter months to turn it into a rink. "You will find an entrance on either side of the house," the rich man wrote. "Put your hand through the gate and pull the bolt."

Less than two years later, unfortunately, sadness struck the Avery family, not once, but twice as Oswald's father and then his older brother Ernest both died in 1892. This left 15-year-old Oswald playing solo on the Mariners' Temple steps, as well as becoming the man of the family and a father figure to little Roy. Elizabeth Avery started working for the Baptist City Mission Society. In the course of her work, she met a number of very wealthy people who took an interest in her two surviving sons and invited the boys to spend time on their large estates away from the city during the summer.

But neither the two deaths nor the "vice in a hundred repulsive forms" in his immediate environment could stop Oswald from graduating from the New York Male Grammar School in 1893. Not long afterward—perhaps with the help of the wealthy people his mother worked with—he moved away from home and enrolled at the Colgate Academy in the village of Hamilton in central New York, about 150 miles from New York City.

College life at that time was much more difficult than it is now. Students had to clean their own rooms and equip themselves with mops, brooms and dustpans. They studied by kerosene lamps, and had to walk down a steep hill from the college to the village of Hamilton to buy all their supplies. During the winter, they made the trip in deep snow. Also, the fire in their dormitory stoves would often go out in the night and the pump—their only source for fresh water— might freeze tight. They couldn't just lie in bed and stay warm because breakfast and classes both began early in the morning.

Despite these difficulties, Oswald made excellent grades, and he continued tooting his cornet as the University's band leader. He also tooted his personal horn as a very good public speaker who won several oratorical contests. Many years later, he still loved to repeat one of his prize-winning speeches about Chinese civilization to his colleagues in the scientific laboratory where he worked, perhaps remembering the excitement that surrounded those contests.

A popular young man, he acquired the affectionate nickname of "Babe" because of his small size—he stood just five feet, two inches. Dubos' biography suggests that his impact among his fellow students was as large as his physical stature was small: "Photographs of him among the other members of the band show a face giving an impression of alertness, intensity, forcefulness, and a touch of youthful arrogance. During his junior year, it was said of him in the yearbook that only the accident of having been born in Halifax and therefore a foreigner prevented him from pursuing 'his aspirations for the Presidency.'"

The would-be predecessor of Ronald Reagan, George Bush and Bill Clinton graduated from Colgate University in 1900 with a Bachelor of Arts degree and a major in the humanities. The man who would make a revolutionary scientific discovery almost half a century later took the bare minimum of science courses, just enough to fill the requirements for graduation. Even in his senior year, none of his courses were in science.

Yet just a few months later, Oswald entered Columbia University College of Physicians and Surgeons in New York City. So the turn of the century found young Oswald tentatively putting his hand through the gate.

Dr. Avery was already in general practice when Sir Almroth Wright, from England, (shown here) crossed his path. From that time, Dr. Avery became very interested in the field of bacteriology.

Chapter 3

Medical School and an Unhappy Doctor

I t's likely that Oswald Avery entered Colgate University intending to follow his father into the ministry, which might explain why he became such a good public speaker. But neither he nor his family ever recorded why he suddenly became interested in medicine.

He may have faced a crisis which triggered this choice. Maybe he remembered his father's "Avery's Auraline" and wanted to help people with a similar drug. Perhaps he wanted to know what caused the deaths of his father and brother. This was also an age of missionaries doing good works, so he may have considered that being a doctor and helping to cure people of diseases was like being a minister in a way. His parents, after all, had given up a secure position in comfortable surroundings in Halifax to perform pastoral work among the "heathen" of New York and their son could well have absorbed that same attitude.

Rene Dubos in his biography of Avery suggests yet another possibility. When Oswald was five, his mother suddenly began running a high fever. She lost consciousness and became stiff and cold. The doctor standing by her bed pronounced her dead. Yet two hours later she suddenly awoke and cried, "I have been dead, have I not? Yes, I remember, Jesus waved me back and said 'Not yet my child.' Oh! How disappointed I was." Although he was certainly glad to have his mother back with him, the incident probably made a strong impression on the youngster.

In addition, medicine was beginning to enjoy a great deal of prestige because of many recent discoveries that raised the possibility of finding treatment and cures for infectious diseases that routinely killed thousands of people every year.

But Dubos, who knew Avery very well because of the many years that the two men spent working side-by-side in the same laboratory, said that "Although Avery loved to tell stories about himself, he avoided conversations of a purely personal nature, in particular those involving his family or the very early years of his life. He probably would have regarded any search into his familial background as an unjustified intrusion into his personal affairs; more, he would have felt that the information thus obtained would not possibly throw useful light on his scientific achievements."

Whatever his reasons for choosing to enter medical school, his lack of science courses wasn't a handicap. First-year students at the College of Physicians and Surgeons normally took courses like physics and chemistry after they enrolled there, rather than as undergraduates as prospective doctors do now.

Avery apparently never spoke of his four years at the College of Physicians and Surgeons, and the only records that remain are his grades. They were almost all good, except for courses in bacteriology and pathology—the two fields in which he would later become famous.

Avery graduated from medical school in 1904, and joined several other doctors who performed what they termed "general surgery," or what we could call today general practice. It turned out to be a frustrating period of his life, for many of his patients suffered from a variety of chronic diseases such as asthma and he could do very little to ease their suffering, let alone cure them.

So it was fortunate for him when an English doctor named Sir Almroth Wright traveled to New York to deliver a lecture at the Academy of Medicine on his recent invention of an opsonic technique.

Opsonins are components of the blood's serum. They act upon invading cells or bacteria to assist in absorbing and destroying them in blood and body tissues to give protection against infectious diseases.

Representatives from the New York City Health Department attended the lecture and became interested in the technique. A colleague of Dr. Wright's was engaged to give a short instructional course to a small group of professionals.

Avery was one of the men selected to take the course. When it was completed, he left private medical practice to take a part-time job compiling opsonic indices for the Board of Health for $50 per month. He also picked up another part-time job doing milk bacteriology for the Sheffield Company. At that time, milk pasteurization on a large-scale basis was just beginning. So Avery conducted bacterial counts of milk before and after pasteurization for another $50 per month. While both jobs were useful in providing him with an income, they weren't long-term or very satisfying.

But as so often happens, it helps to know the right person.

While he was studying at Colgate, Avery had shared a room with William M. Parke. After graduation, Avery moved back home with his mother, who had by this time left the slums of the Lower East Side. Parke, now attending law school, joined them.

When Parke graduated from law school and passed his bar exam, he began his legal practice in the same building where a man named Benjamin White happened to live. White had earned a Ph.D. in physiological chemistry from Yale University in 1903 and four years later was appointed director of the Hoagland Laboratory in Brooklyn, a privately funded institution that performed bacteriological research.

The three men, all bachelors, became friends and White soon told Avery that he needed a young doctor to serve as an assistant director at the Hoagland Laboratory. Holding just his two part-time positions, Avery was enthusiastic about the job and was quickly hired at an annual salary of $1,200. Though it only matched what he was already earning, the job had much more responsibility and much greater prospects for advancement, all the more so because of White's background. He helped his new assistant to learn advanced laboratory techniques and vastly broadened his knowledge of chemistry.

Dr. Avery and his colleagues taking a photo break at their laboratory in the Rockefeller Institute of Medicine, which later became Rockefeller University.

Dr. Avery was known for his humility, kindness, and temperance.

Chapter 4
Hoagland Laboratory

Avery's new place of employment was founded in 1888 by Cornelius Hoagland, who had been a physician before amassing a considerable fortune selling baking soda. But in 1884 his grandson died of diphtheria—a disease common at that time that was caused by a bacterial infection—and the tragedy caused Hoagland to donate much of his money to founding a laboratory that would advance the study of medical bacteriology.

Avery began by collaborating with White on a study of the bacteriology of yogurt and other types of fermented milk. Some researchers believed that these products helped people live longer by controlling harmful bacteria in the intestines and therefore reducing the risk of disease. While the study itself was not of great importance, it helped introduce Avery to laboratory research.

Hoagland also offered him a chance to use the oratorical skills he'd developed at Colgate, because one of his duties was to teach a course for student nurses. He quickly acquired the nicknames that followed him through the rest of his professional career. At first he was known as "The Professor," and then, more fondly, as "Fess."

But his main purpose for being at Hoagland was to conduct research. He and White worked together on a number of medical issues. As a result Avery received a great deal of training and practical experience in various areas of bacteriology and immunology. His research findings led to him publishing nine scientific papers during the six years that he spent at Hoagland.

One of them, entitled "Opsonins and Vaccine Therapy," was published in *Hare's Modern Treatment*, one of the most frequently used medical textbooks of that era.

But in terms of his future, the most important was one that resulted from a study he undertook beginning in 1910. White contracted a serious case of tuberculosis and went to a sanitarium in the Adirondack mountains. Avery accompanied him during his initial visit, and returned several times later to conduct systematic clinical studies on patients there. The report of his findings, "Concerning secondary infection in pulmonary tuberculosis," was published in the *Journal of Medical Research* in 1913.

One man who read the paper with special interest was Dr. Rufus Cole, the director of the hospital of The Rockefeller Institute for Medical Research in New York City. When the hospital opened in 1910, Cole and his team of scientists were given a list of several major infectious diseases to study, including polio, syphilis and heart disease. Cole chose to study lobar pneumonia, which resulted in more deaths than any of the others. Caused by a bacteria known as pneumococcus, lobar pneumonia killed at least 20% of the people who caught it—more than 50,000 people every year in the United States alone.

Though Cole's team made quick progress in the beginning in their efforts to develop a serum that would be effective against pneumonia, they encountered a major problem: There were actually several different types, or strains, of the pneumococcus bacteria, and each would require a different serum. They needed to be able to analyze the slightly different chemical composition of each of the various strains. For their further investigations, therefore, they needed someone who was familiar with bacteriology and immunology—and understood chemistry.

Then Cole ran across Avery's paper on tuberculosis. Believing that it revealed precisely the ability to conduct a systematic investigation in a clinical environment that he needed, Cole drove over to Brooklyn and met Avery at the Hoagland Laboratory.

By that time, Avery's research had shifted to pneumococcus, likely in part because his mother had died of the pneumonia in 1910. That made Avery even more attractive to Cole, who was so impressed that he urged the director of the Rockefeller Institute, Dr. Simon Flexner, to invite Avery to lunch at the Rockefeller Institute. After meeting Avery, Flexner was also impressed. The two men mailed Avery a job offer as a bacteriologist at the hospital.

He didn't reply. Flexner mailed Avery a second time. Still no reply.

So Cole drove over to Brooklyn again, this time with a better offer. He discovered that Avery hadn't ignored them because the financial incentives weren't enough. He was just too busy to reply. And he was happy where he was.

Avery did accept the offer and now, nearly thirty-seven years old, left Hoagland. He had demonstrated great concentration and persistence when working on his various projects, he was thorough and very logical in his deductions, and he was very persistent. These abilities would hold throughout his career and add to his stature as a bacteriologist.

Avery said that Hoagland had been "a wonderful place for a young man to get his start," according to Arnold Eggerth's *History of the Hoagland Laboratory.*

Little did he realize that he was going to the place where he would finish his career.

When the call came from Uncle Sam during World War I, Dr. Avery wanted to do his part. Here he's in his private's uniform. Later he became a captain.

Chapter 5

Pulling the Bolt

●●●

Interestingly, The Rockefeller Institute, of which the hospital where Avery was hired was a part, had also been founded because of the death of a grandson. In this case, it was the grandson of John D. Rockefeller, who had been involved in Avery's life a quarter of a century earlier because of his donations to the Mariners' Temple—and that long-ago invitation to go ice skating in his back yard.

John Rockefeller McCormick was just three when he died of scarlet fever in 1903, and his grieving grandfather was shocked to learn that not only was there no treatment for the disease, no one even knew what caused it. In less than a year, John D. Rockefeller had provided the necessary funds to open the Institute and enable it to begin an ambitious program of medical research.

Avery's laboratory work was interrupted in 1917 when the US entered World War I. Avery wanted to volunteer and become a commissioned officer in the US Army, which was customary for doctors. But even though he had lived in the country for 30 years, he was still technically a British subject because he had never taken the time to become a naturalized citizen. He was therefore not eligible to become an officer.

So he enlisted in the army as a private. His military service eventually led to his being naturalized in 1918, which in turn meant that he could be an officer. Soon after becoming a citizen, he received a promotion to captain.

But before that happened he often lectured about bacteriology and infectious diseases to groups of officers. At first the captains, majors and colonels were startled that this small, 40-year-old private would be trying to tell them what to do. But they quickly recognized that he knew what he was talking about. It was, however, the last time that he lectured on a formal, regular basis.

By then, he had also settled into the pattern of living that he retained for the rest of his time at the Institute. He roomed with another researcher at the Institute, Dr. A.R. Dochez. The two men had a Danish housekeeper named Elsa who cooked and cleaned for them. "Fess" and "Do" would sometimes have younger members of the Rockefeller Institute living with them for brief periods.

While he was immensely popular and well-liked by his colleagues, Avery rarely accepted any of the many social invitations he received. His work and his commitment to his research was total. But one of the reasons for his popularity was that he never lorded it over the people he worked with.

Dubos writes that "Avery's own laboratory was the smallest; it had formerly been the ward kitchen, and was equipped with the barest of bacteriological necessities. His office was adjacent to his laboratory and was, like it, small and bare. Both rooms were neat and clean, but kept as empty as possible, without the photographs, pictures, momentos, unused books and other friendly items that usually adorn and clutter the working places of the white-collar class. The austerity of his office and laboratory symbolized how much he had given up in all aspects of his life for the sake of utter concentration on a few chosen goals."

In pursuit of those goals, he went down more than a few blind alleys, which is common in scientific research. His dogged persistence led to many important discoveries about the nature of pneumococcus, especially during the 1920s.

"We have forgotten," wrote F.M. Burnet in his book *War-Time Visit to America*, "that pneumonia was once the 'captain of the men of death' but for the period between the two wars the study of pneumonia and the other pneumococcal infections was the most active and successful area of bacteriological research. The Rockefeller Institute was the world center for that research and over the whole period Avery was its guiding spirit though he had many brilliant collaborators."

By 1921, Avery and his associates had identified four strains of pneumococcus (called Types I, II, III and IV) and were well advanced in developing a Type I serum. They had also learned that the virulence, or degree of harmfulness, of each type was related to the external capsule that the bacteria developed. This capsule was a smooth sort of gelatin that surrounded virulent pneumococcus bacteria. If it wasn't present, the outside of the bacteria was "rough" and it was harmless.

Avery termed the substance a "specific soluable substance," SSS for short, and devoted his major effort to learning its chemical composition. Surprisingly, it turned out to be polysaccharides—complex structures of different kinds of sugar molecules. Consequently, Avery nicknamed pneumococcus the "sugar-coated microbe."

But there was nothing sweet about pneumonia, the disease it caused. Avery's discovery aided in the development of the different kinds of sera which would be effective against each strain.

The austerity of Dr. Avery's "office and laboratory symbolized how much he had given up in all aspects of his life for the sake of utter concentration on a few chosen goals."

Chapter 6
The Transforming Principle

• •

I t took another researcher to begin what would become Oswald Avery's most famous contribution to medical science. In 1923, Dr. Fred Griffith, a British researcher, proved that each of the different strains of pneumococcal types could exist as either R (rough) or S (smooth) forms. This fit perfectly with what Avery had also discovered, that bacteria which had lost their smooth capsules became harmless, while those that still had them were harmful.

Five years later, Griffith discovered something disturbing. He began by injecting mice with virulent (S) pneumococcus bacteria. The mice died. Then he injected non-virulent (R) pneumococcus into another group of mice. These survived. So did the third group, mice that were injected with virulent bacteria that had been heat-treated to kill the live bacteria.

Then he injected a combination of non-virulent bacteria of Type I and heat-killed bacteria of Type II into mice and they all died. By themselves, neither had been lethal. Griffith's next step was to isolate the harmful, living encapsulated bacteria from the corpses. While it wasn't entirely surprising that the mice had died, what astonished Griffith was that the living pneumococcus bacteria he recovered from the corpses were not Type I as he had expected—the original living strain—but Type II. Even more, the newly formed Type II continued to grow as Type II when he put them into a culture medium. Somehow the change had become hereditary; Type I had been altered into Type II.

A cautious man by nature, Griffith nevertheless claimed that "a transforming principle" from the dead encapsulated (S) bacteria caused capsule development in the living, unencapsulated (R) bacteria, making them harmful. Somehow, the dead strain was giving the previously harmless strain something to make it lethal.

This report didn't appear logical to other scientists, including Avery, even though Griffith enjoyed an excellent reputation in the scientific community for the extreme care with which he conducted his experiments. In fact, Avery initially dismissed the findings. But when later studies, including one in 1931 at Rockefeller, confirmed Griffith's report, Avery and his colleague Dr. Colin MacLeod started their own investigation into the nature of what by then was known as the "transforming principle."

It took nearly a decade for the project to kick into high gear. Avery contracted Graves' disease soon after beginning the search for the transforming principle. That is a condition in which the thyroid gland becomes enlarged and although he tried to conceal his illness, it left him subject to fits of irritation and excitability. Finally he had his thyroid removed and spent several months recuperating. In addition, the researchers encountered technical problems. And the hospital had other commitments, including the ongoing desire to develop sera effective against the other types of pneumonia.

But the development of antibiotics which were effective against pneumonia in the late 1930s made it possible for Avery and MacLeod—who by now had been joined by Dr. Maclyn McCarty—to devote their primary efforts to transformation in the early 1940s. The subsequent research took a little less than two years.

Expressed in simple terms (though the methods the men employed were anything but simple), the experiment was primarily a process of elimination. The researchers began with the assumption that something in the bacteria was responsible for the transformation. They just didn't know what it was.

So one by one, they destroyed different substances occurring within the virulent pneumococcus bacteria. If the transformation from harmless to harmful still occurred, that meant that that particular substance could not be the transforming principle.

First they obtained a pure sample of the harmful, living, encapsulated bacteria. Then they killed it by heat treatment. The bacteria's polysaccharide (a sugar) and protein (which makes up the capsule and is also found in the cells) were removed. What the scientists had left was added to living, unencapsulated bacteria.

Then the bacteria reproduced. Their offspring had capsules. This meant the active transforming principle still remained. So it was neither a protein nor a polysaccharide.

They eliminated several other possibilities as well. Then they destroyed the DNA. Transformation didn't occur. They had discovered the transforming substance.

Their analysis proved that DNA, deoxyribonucleic acid, was the transforming principle responsible for the development of polysaccharide capsules in the previously unencapsulated bacteria.

No doubt Dr. Avery and his colleagues were surprised by the discovery, yet they were strongly convinced that deoxyribonucleic acid was the true transforming principle which held the secrets of life. The Royal Society in England awarded the Copley Medal to Dr. Avery in 1945 for his work.

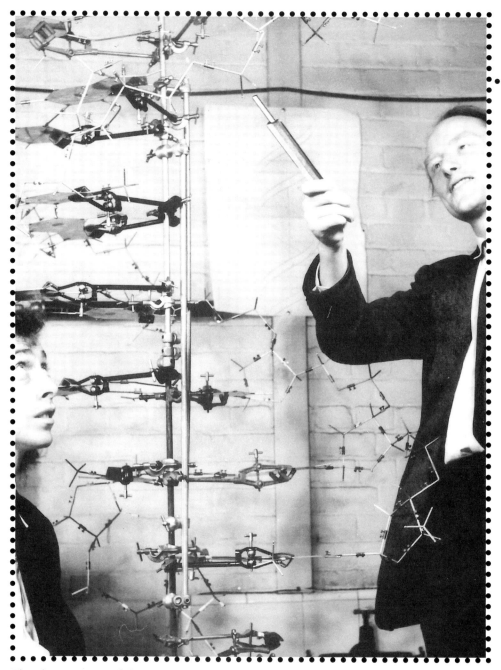

The discoverers of the structure of DNA, James Watson (left) and Francis Crick are shown with their model of part of a DNA molecule in 1953. Crick and Watson met at the Cavendish Laboratory in Cambridge in 1951. The two shared a Nobel Prize for Physiology in 1962 with Maurice Wilkins.

Chapter 7
Disappointment Deluxe

• •

Today, we take it for granted that DNA is the carrier of genetic information. But when Avery and his colleagues published their paper, things were very different. For many years, the prevailing belief had been that protein, rather than DNA, carried genetic material. Protein has twenty different subunits compared with just four for DNA, which seemed to make it much more diverse and therefore far more capable of holding a vast amount of genetic information. In fact, many scientists considered DNA "boring" and it was a long-shot at best. It was so little studied that no one even knew exactly what it looked like.

So it wasn't entirely surprising that even though Avery, McCarty and MacLeod phrased their conclusions rather cautiously, a number of scientists questioned their conclusions. They were accused of errors in both their experimental methods and chemical analysis.

Some of the harshest criticism came from their colleagues at the Rockefeller Institute. Dr. P.A. Levene was considered the world's foremost expert on DNA, and he considered that it was too simple a substance to be the transforming principle. He therefore maintained that the material that Avery and his colleagues had used had somehow become contaminated. Another opponent was Dr. Alfred Mirsky, who had long believed that a particular type of proteins called nucleoproteins were responsible for carrying genetic information.

There was another problem as well: over the years, Avery had become such a soft-spoken, modest man that it was hard for him to be forward in pushing his accomplishment.

Franklin Stahl's *We Can Sleep Later* notes that Dr. Alfred Hershey, who would later supply definitive proof for Avery's conclusion, "felt that Dr. Avery and the others were just 'too modest.' He also felt they should have done more 'advertising', talking about their discovery and presenting it in various places."

Stahl also notes that "A Polish scientist, Waclaw Szybalski, who later came to America to work, wondered why the American scientists didn't believe in Avery's work when those in Poland did. Szybalski had read 'the very convincing chemical and enzymatic data on the DNA nature of the transforming principle' in the *Journal of Experimental Medicine*.

"Dr. Hershey replied, 'Maybe you in Poland believed Avery's 1944 data, but nobody in America believed their data because Mirsky convinced everybody that Avery did not know the difference between the nucleoproteins, which must be the essence of transforming principle, and the DNA."

One result from all this negative fallout was that even though Avery, MacLeod and McCarty were nominated for the Nobel Prize, the selection committee declined to award it to them. As Dubos stated in his obituary of Avery in the *Biographical Memoirs of the Royal Society* in 1956, "it remains to this day, a matter of painful surprise that Avery was not awarded a Nobel Prize."

A.G. Bearn in *Perspectives in Biology and Medicine* says that "The surprise Dubos expressed still remains. The discovery that DNA was the genetic material remains the most fundamental biological discovery of the 20th century."

Others shared similar sentiments about the importance of Avery's discovery.

"The identification of the 'transforming principle' was wonderful and still is wonderful," said Hershey in 1953, as quoted in *We Can Sleep Later*.

And Burnet lauded Dr. Avery in his book, *War-time Visit to America*, with these words: "At the Rockefeller Institute I called on O.T. Avery who, in the words of a letter of mine: 'has just made an extremely exciting discovery which, put rather crudely, is nothing less than the isolation of a pure gene in the form of deoxyribonucleic acid.' Nothing since has diminished the significance or importance of Avery's work."

Avery, who had already been past the normal retirement age when he discovered the transforming principle, left the Rockefeller Institute in 1948. He was 71. He said goodbye to his longtime colleagues and moved out of the apartment he'd shared with Dr. Dochez for so many years.

Avery settled in Nashville, Tennessee to be near his brother Roy, who taught bacteriology at Vanderbilt University School of Medicine. He found an old stone house just a few doors away from Roy and the two men spent considerable time together on an almost daily basis. His cousin Minnie Wandell served as his housekeeper.

But in 1954, during his customary summer visit to Deer Isle, he experienced some stomach discomfort. He was soon diagnosed with cancer of the liver. Following a painful illness, Dr. Oswald Theodore Avery died on February 20, 1955. Ironically, it was the anniversary of the date of Alfred Nobel's death.

This photo of Dr. Avery (left) was taken in 1947 after he accepted the Lasker Award in New York City.

Chapter 8
After Avery's Discovery

Despite the initial reservations, it didn't take long for scientists who followed Avery to prove him correct and build on his discovery. DNA molecules were no longer "boring."

In 1952 Dr. Hershey and his assistant Martha Chase conducted experiments at the Cold Spring Harbor Laboratory in New York which proved that only DNA entered bacterial cells, and that it—and it alone—carries the genetic message for replication. Their work proved to be definitive and silenced virtually all of the remaining skeptics. But no one still really knew what it looked like.

So the next challenge was to determine the detailed structure of DNA.

Scientists already knew that its four subunits were the bases Adenine, Thymine, Cytosine and Guanine. Dr. Edwin Chargaff and his colleagues discovered in 1950 that the amount of Adenine always equals the Thymine amount, and that Cytosine and Guanine also occur in identical amounts. In its simplest form, you could say that A=T and G=C, which became known as Chargaff's Rule. The significance of this finding had to wait several years, however.

The next clue came from the crystallography studies of British biophysicists Maurice Wilkins and Rosalind Franklin. They obtained an x-ray pattern of DNA that appeared to consist of two vertical strands joined together by a series of rungs, with the resulting ladder-like structure then twisted into the form of a helix.

The pieces came together when a young American Ph.D. named James Watson hooked up in London, England with Francis Crick, an older British researcher who was working on his doctorate. The two men used cutout cardboard shapes based on the findings of Wilkins and Franklin to work out possible chemical bonds among the four bases, which formed the rungs. Two of the bases, Adenine and Guanine, were known as purines, with two carbon-nitrogen rings in their structures. The other two, Thymine and Cytosine, known as pyrimidines, had one such ring. So if the bases were paired up so that the purines and pyrimidines were linked with each other, the resulting DNA would quickly become ungainly and lopsided. So they paired Adenine (purine) with Thymine (pyrimidine) and Guanine (purine) with Cytosine (pyrimidine) and the resulting structure became uniform—which also accords with Chargaff's Rule.

So their final model turned out to be two spirals of DNA joined together by the two combinations of bases to create a double helix. The actual chemical structure of DNA is identical for everyone. The difference among people (and therefore the validity of DNA fingerprinting) is the order in which the millions of base pairs occur. Every person has a different sequence.

Crick, Watson and Wilkins shared a Nobel Prize in 1962 for their work. Franklin, unfortunately, had died by that time.

Let's look at some of the current uses for DNA which touch the lives of many people.

• Sheldon was 15 and had never seen his father. When other boys brought their fathers to school, Sheldon brought his mother, and sometimes his grandmother. Sheldon seldom mentioned his missing father, but often wondered about him. When his mother began working for the Department of Human Services, she asked them to hunt for Sheldon's father, Greg. It took a while, but they found him. Greg asked for and was granted a DNA test to prove he was the father of Sheldon. The results satisfied everyone that Greg and Sheldon are father and son.

• DNA testing is so accurate that it can be used to match tissues in organ donation and diagnose specific viral diseases.

• DNA fingerprinting originated in 1984 as the result of research conducted by Dr. Alec Jeffries of the Lister Institute of Leicester University in England. As we saw in the example in Chapter 1, it has resulted in the release of people wrongfully convicted of crimes, as well as providing proof of guilt in many cases. Jeffries was later knighted by the Queen for his accomplishments.

• Most people are familiar with the Unknown Soldier who is buried in a tomb at Arlington National Cemetery in Washington, D.C. But now, unidentified and missing soldiers whose bodies are returned from Vietnam and Korea can be identified through DNA testing.

• A teacher in Cheddar, England was proved to be a direct descendant of a person whose 9000-year-old bones were found in a nearby cave.

• Yellow roses can be created by making changes in the DNA of red roses.

• Couples who might have inherited diseases which are passed down from one generation to another can be tested prior to marriage to identify the location on their DNA string of the gene which carries the disease. In the future, some of these situations hopefully can be corrected by doctors when the child is born, or soon thereafter.

• Many diabetic teenagers must take insulin daily because their bodies are unable to manufacture sufficient amounts. Scientists can take a portion of DNA from a body which produces plenty of insulin to splice into bacterial DNA. Then the bacteria can be grown in large quantities to produce insulin. Once it is extracted, the insulin is ready for use by diabetics.

• Not long ago, researchers made headlines when they produced a cloned sheep named Dolly.

All these developments can be traced back to Avery.

"According to other scientists, all of biology today is based on Avery's 1944 paper," says a 1998 online press release announcing the creation of a website produced by the National Library of Medicine called Profiles in Science. "Dr. Paul A. Marks, president of the Sloan-Kettering Cancer Center, says, 'The discovery that DNA is hereditary material is perhaps the most important discovery in biology of the 20th century.' Sir Peter Medawar, a Nobel winner, calls Avery's research 'The most interesting and portentous biological experiment of the 20th century.'" So it's not surprising that Avery was the first scientist to be included in this new online resource.

Rockefeller Institute, which eventually became Rockefeller University, has not forgotten the small man who made such a large contribution to the scientific world. A massive granite gateway in his name stands at the northwest corner of the campus.

Soon after he retired as director of the Rockefeller Institute in 1935, Simon Flexner wrote a letter to Avery which captures both the personal and professional esteem in which he was held and his lasting contribution to science:

"I regard it as one of the pieces of the greatest good fortune for the Institute that you came there so early in the Hospital's history and are still there to carry on your most important and original work, which no one else could possibly have done as you have done it. There is no one that I got more pleasure and stimulation in talking with than yourself. It was one of my privileges to have this understanding, intimate relation with you."

Oswald Avery Chronology

- 1877, born on October 21 to Joseph and Elizabeth Avery in Halifax, Nova Scotia
- 1887, moves with family to New York City, where his father becomes pastor at the Baptist Mariners' Temple
- 1892, Oswald's father and oldest brother, Ernest, both die
- 1896, graduates from Colgate Academy
- 1900, graduates from Colgate University with an A.B. degree
- 1904, receives M.D. degree from College of Physicians and Surgeons of Columbia University, New York
- 1907, begins working at Hoagland Laboratory in Brooklyn where he becomes Associate Director of the Division of Bacteriology
- 1913, joins staff of Rockefeller Hospital by invitation of director Rufus Cole
- 1918, becomes naturalized US citizen
- 1923, becomes member of the Rockefeller Institute for Medical Research, where he makes many discoveries
- 1933, elected to the National Academy of Sciences in America
- 1941, elected President of the Society of American Bacteriologists
- 1943, becomes member emeritus of Rockefeller Institute
- 1944, publishes results of research with Colin MacLeod and Maclyn McCarty on the transforming principle
- 1944, named a foreign member of the Royal Society of London
- 1944, awarded Gold Medal by the New York Academy of Medicine
- 1945, receives the Copley Medal from the Royal Society of London
- 1947, receives the Lasker Award from the American Public Health Association
- 1948, retires to Nashville, Tennessee
- 1950, awarded Pasteur Gold Medal by Swedish Medical Society
- 1955, dies of liver cancer in Nashville, Tennessee on February 20
- 1965, Avery Memorial Gateway dedicated at Rockefeller University

DNA Timeline

- **1665**, English scientist Robert Hooke observes cork cross-section through his microscope and notes that it is composed of tiny rectangular divisions. He names them "cells," after the small rooms in monasteries.
- **1724**, discovery of cross-fertilization in corn, first "genetic engineering" project
- **1831**, Scottish botanist Robert Brown notes that all cells have small, dark structure in their center. He names it "nucleus," Latin for "little nut."
- **1838**, German scientist Matthias Schleiden concludes that all plants are composed of cells.
- **1839**, German scientist Theodor Schwann determines that all animals are composed of cells.
- **1866**, Silesian monk Gregor Mendel publishes *Experiments with Plant Hybrids*,
- **1868**, Swiss biologist Friedrich Miescher discovers DNA, which he calls "nuclein"
- **1879**, German scientist Walther Flemming discovers chromosomes
- **1887**, Belgian botanist Eduard von Beneden notes that each type of plant or animal has the same number of chromosomes. (Different organisms have different numbers of chromosomes; for example, humans have 46 and fruit flies have 4.)
- **1892**, German scientist August Weissmann proposes that parent reproductive cells contain information telling their offspring how to develop
- **1903**, US scientist Walter Sutton shows that chromosomes come in pairs
- **1905**, US scientist Edmund Wilson proposes that separate X and Y chromosomes determine sex; single Y chromosome means maleness and two X chromosomes say "it's a girl!"
- **1909**, Danish botanist Wilhelm Johannsen gives name of "genes" to the sections of chromosomes that carry material that passes traits from one generation to another
- **1944**, Oswald Avery and colleagues demonstrate that DNA is transforming principle
- **1953**, American scientist James Watson and British scientist Francis Crick demonstrate "double helix" structure of DNA
- **1984**, British scientist Alec Jeffries invents DNA fingerprinting
- **1997**, cloning of Dolly the sheep
- **2000**, sequencing of entire human genome completed

Glossary

Bacteriology - branch of biology and medicine dealing with bacteria.

Biochemistry - branch of chemistry dealing with processes and physical properties of living organisms.

DNA - Deoxyribonucleic acid, a nucleic acid that consists of two long chains of nucleotides twisted together into a double helix and joined by hydrogen bonds between complementary bases adenine and thymine or cytosine and guanine. It carries the cell's genetic information and hereditary characteristics via its nucleotides and their sequences and is capable of being replicated and serving as a template for RNA synthesis.

DNA fingerprinting - A method used to identify multilocus DNA fragment banding patterns that are specific to an individual by exposing a sample of the person's DNA to enzymatic digestion and various analytical techniques such as Southern blot analysis.

Double Helix - Two threads of DNA which are held together by complementary bases (Cytosine and Guanine or Adenine and Thymine) forming two parallel helices which encode the sequences of genes.

Helix - A line, thread, wire, or the like, curved into a shape such as it would assume if wound in a single layer around a cylinder.

Hemolytic streptococcus - a streptococcus that produces a toxin which causes red blood cells' destruction.

Leukocyte - A white or colorless blood cell, constituting an important agent in protection against infectious diseases.

Lysis - the bursting or opening of a cell.

Microbiology - branch of biology which studies microscopic microorganisms.

Opsonin - a component of blood serum that acts upon invading cells or bacteria to assist in their absorption by phagocytes.

Phagocytes - leukocyte that ingests and destroys harmful bacteria in blood and body tissues

Physiology - study of the processes and mechanisms by which animals and plants function under varied conditions.

Polysaccharides - Poly- means many; saccharides a large group of carbohydrates containing sugar.

Sensitivity - capacity of an organ or organisms to respond to a stimulus.

Serology - the science of serums and their actions.

Serum - clear, slightly yellow portion of the body's liquid after separation of its solid elements, especially that formed by the clotting of blood.

Syndrome - group of symptoms that collectively indicate or characterize a disease, a psychological disorder or another abnormal condition.

Virulent - having the power to injure an organism by invasion of tissue and generation of internal toxins, as do certain microorganisms.

Further Reading

Books for advanced readers:

de Kruif, Paul. *Microbe Hunters*. Pleasantville, NY, Readers Digest
    Association, 1962.

Dubos, René. *The Professor, the Institute, and DNA*. New York, The
    Rockefeller University Press, 1956.

Dwyer, Jim, Barry Scheck, and Peter Neufeld. *Actual Innocence*. New York:
    Doubleday, 2000.

Eggerth, Arnold H. *History of The Hoagland Laboratory*, Brooklyn, N.Y.,
    1960.

Wilcox, Frank H. *DNA: The Thread Of Life*. Lerner Publications Company,
    1988.

Websites:

http://www.profiles.nlm.nih.gov/CC/

Index